Janet Carlson Calvert Library
5 Tyler Drive
Franklin, CT 06254

W9-BFE-574

DATE DUE

J
614
.549
HAR

PERSPECTIVES ON
AMERICAN PROGRESS

THE DISCOVERY
OF THE
POLIO VACCINE

BY DUCHESS HARRIS, JD, PHD

WITH HEATHER C. HUDAK

Core Library

Cover image: Jonas Salk worked for years to develop a
vaccine for polio.

An Imprint of Abdo Publishing
abdopublishing.com

abdopublishing.com

Published by Abdo Publishing, a division of ABDO, PO Box 398166,
Minneapolis, Minnesota 55439. Copyright © 2019 by Abdo Consulting
Group, Inc. International copyrights reserved in all countries. No part of this
book may be reproduced in any form without written permission from the
publisher. Core Library™ is a trademark and logo of Abdo Publishing.

Printed in the United States of America, North Mankato, Minnesota
042018
092018

THIS BOOK CONTAINS
RECYCLED MATERIALS

Cover Photo: Bettmann/Getty Images
Interior Photos: Bettmann/Getty Images, 1, 26–27; Everett Collection/Newscom, 4–5, 29; Henry
Griffin/AP Images, 6; Red Line Editorial, 7, 38; Picture History/Newscom, 9; The Herald Bulletin/
AP Images, 12; akg-images/Newscom, 16–17; AP Images, 19, 33; UPPA/Photoshot/Newscom, 21;
World History Archive/Newscom, 31; Sunday Alamba/AP Images, 36–37

Editor: Claire Vanden Branden
Imprint Designer: Maggie Villaume
Series Design Direction: Ryan Gale

Library of Congress Control Number: 2017962648

Publisher's Cataloging-in-Publication Data

Names: Harris, Duchess, author. | Hudak, Heather C., author.
Title: The discovery of the Polio vaccine / by Duchess Harris and Heather C. Hudak.
Description: Minneapolis, Minnesota : Abdo Publishing, 2019. | Series: Perspectives on American
    progress | Includes online resources and index.
Identifiers: ISBN 9781532114885 (lib.bdg.) | ISBN 9781532154713 (ebook)
Subjects: LCSH: Vaccines--Juvenile literature. | Poliomyelitis--Juvenile literature. | Virology--
    Juvenile literature. | Vaccination of children--United States—Juvenile literature.
Classification: DDC 614.549--dc23

CONTENTS

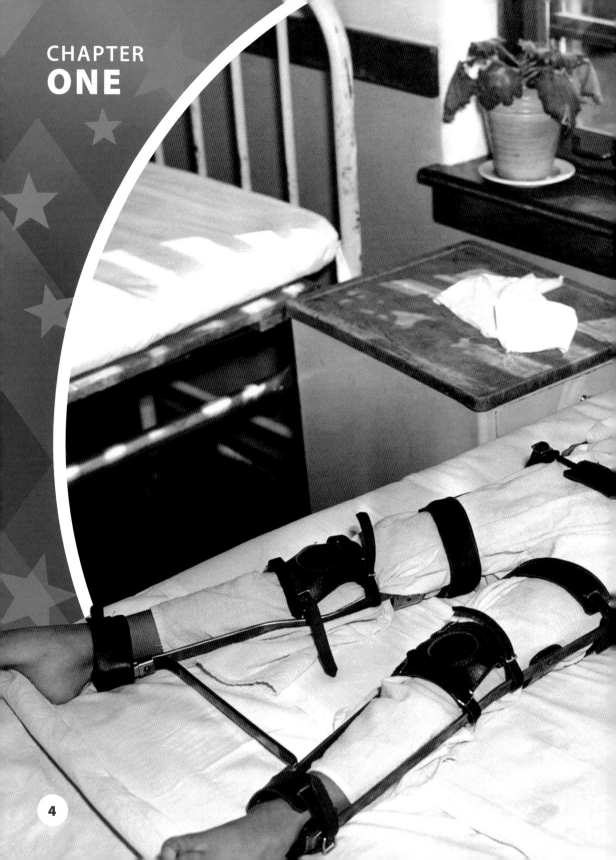

A DEADLY DISEASE GRIPS AMERICA

For most, summertime means warm weather, beaches, family trips, and fun. But in the early 1900s, it brought fears of a deadly disease called poliomyelitis. The disease is better known as polio. It strikes the central nervous system. It attacks the brain and spinal cord. It can cause paralysis or even death. Polio spreads easily through person-to-person contact. Tens of thousands of Americans were infected with polio in the first half of the 1900s.

Polio victims often used leg braces to help their weak muscles.

Jonas Salk, *left*, and Albert Sabin, *right*, dedicated their careers to finding a cure for polio. Later on, their discoveries would help find answers to other diseases.

The first major polio epidemic in the United States took place in 1894. By the 1910s, it was widespread across the country. People feared for their lives. They were very worried about their children. The disease seemed to target the young. It left hundreds of thousands of children paralyzed each year. In reality,

EARLY STATS, FACTS, AND FIGURES

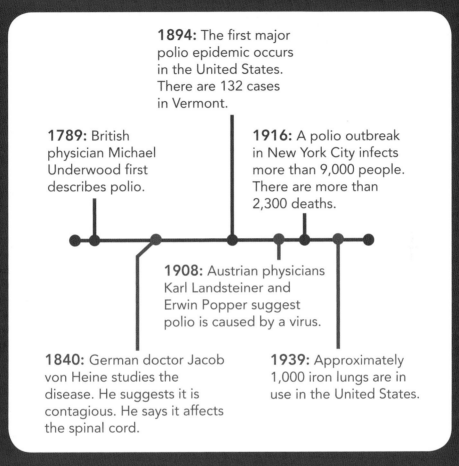

1894: The first major polio epidemic occurs in the United States. There are 132 cases in Vermont.

1789: British physician Michael Underwood first describes polio.

1916: A polio outbreak in New York City infects more than 9,000 people. There are more than 2,300 deaths.

1908: Austrian physicians Karl Landsteiner and Erwin Popper suggest polio is caused by a virus.

1840: German doctor Jacob von Heine studies the disease. He suggests it is contagious. He says it affects the spinal cord.

1939: Approximately 1,000 iron lungs are in use in the United States.

Polio has been known to medical science for more than 200 years. Above is a brief timeline of the disease before a vaccine was discovered. Why might it have taken so long between polio's discovery and its cure?

no one was safe from the grips of the deadly virus. Young or old, rich or poor, polio did not discriminate against its victims.

When the body is attacked with a disease, the immune system fights against it with the help of antibodies. A kind of medicine called a vaccine can also be given to help. A vaccine is a weakened form of the disease. When a vaccine is given, it trains the immune system to defend against the disease. Then if the full-strength disease comes, the immune system knows how to fight to get it out of the body.

Researchers in North America and Europe worked hard to find a cure for polio. Two American scientists, Jonas Salk and Albert Sabin, raced against the clock—and each other—to make a vaccine. Hope came in the spring of 1953. On March 26, Salk announced he had successfully tested a polio vaccine.

Understanding the Disease

The polio virus is highly contagious. It spreads through contact with feces that is infected with the virus. It can also spread through contact with objects, such as toys,

President Franklin D. Roosevelt was a strong advocate for polio victims.

that have been near infected feces. Polio is most often spread through contaminated water. This is common in nations that do not have access to running water or flush toilets. Waste often pollutes water in these places.

The polio virus can live for a long time outside of the human body. Anyone living with someone who has polio will likely get it, too. This is a big problem in parts of the world where there are crowded living conditions. If one person gets polio, it can quickly spread. Children under the age of five and people with poor immune systems are most at risk for polio.

Polio enters a person's body through the nose or mouth. It infects these areas right away. Then it moves to the intestines. Here, it grows quickly. Sometimes it moves on to the immune system or even into the blood. If that happens, it can spread throughout the body. It can attack the central nervous system.

Polio symptoms include sore throat, fever, headache, vomiting, and being very tired. Symptoms last for up to ten days. More than 95 percent of people who have polio show no symptoms. They never even know they have it. But they can still pass it on to other people.

Less than one percent of people who have polio become paralyzed. Symptoms of paralysis include loss of reflexes, floppy limbs, muscle pain, and spasms. In very rare cases, polio attacks the muscles that help people breathe. This can cause death.

Public Impact

In 1946, President Harry S. Truman

HOW A VIRUS SPREADS

There are many different types of viruses. Colds and flus are some of the most common illnesses caused by viruses. Others include hepatitis and polio. Some viruses spread when a person breathes the same air as a person who has the virus or touches an object that person has sneezed or coughed on. Some viruses are passed through skin-to-skin contact. Others are passed by contact with infected blood or body fluids. Some animals and insects carry viruses such as rabies. They are spread to humans through bites.

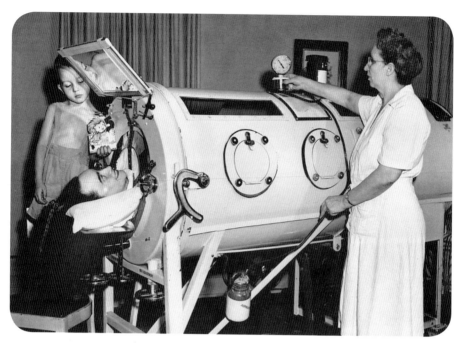

The iron lung was an artificial respirator for polio victims. It was a metal chamber with a bed inside. The machine helped pump air in and out of patients' lungs.

issued a statement. He declared a war on polio. He told people to do whatever they had to do to stop the deadly disease.

Hospitals did not know how to treat polio victims. Some just treated the symptoms. Others turned patients away. Some hospitals put patients in quarantine. If they were having trouble breathing, patients were put inside a machine called an iron lung.

Most polio victims survived. Some people found it difficult to walk. Others needed crutches or wheelchairs. Their lives were changed forever by the disease.

Finding a Solution

People began raising money to find a cure for polio. Early attempts to find a vaccine failed. One attempt caused many deaths. Another gave no defense against the disease. In 1938, President Franklin D. Roosevelt started the National Foundation for Infantile Paralysis (NFIP). Infantile paralysis was another name for polio. The organization held events to raise money for polio research. Money started pouring in for the cause.

Doctors and researchers scrambled to find a cure. Some worked on live virus vaccines. They were made from a form of the virus that had been weakened in a lab. Live virus vaccines provided total immunity. And people who took them no longer carried the virus. Then they could not spread it. Only one dose was needed to become immune. But there was a small

FRANKLIN D. ROOSEVELT

In August 1921, Franklin D. Roosevelt was diagnosed with polio. He started having symptoms when he was 39 years old. Roosevelt was active in politics. His wife, Eleanor, thought he should still pursue his dream. He wanted to become president of the United States. At first, Roosevelt could not campaign. Eleanor gave speeches and went to events on his behalf. Roosevelt became stronger over time. Still, he never completely recovered. In 1928, he became governor of New York. In 1932 he was elected president.

chance the virus could infect the person. Still, many people believed this vaccine was the best option. The only problem was that it was taking a long time for researchers to develop. People wanted a cure fast.

Other researchers worked on killed virus vaccines. The virus was killed using chemicals or heat. Some scientists thought it was less risky than a live virus vaccine. There was no chance it could infect a person. But a person needed more than one dose to become immune. They also needed boosters, or extra doses, later in life. The killed virus vaccine provided immunity. But the person could still carry the virus. Researchers thought it would be faster to develop a killed virus vaccine. They were right.

Jonas Salk studied killed virus vaccines. At the same time, Albert Sabin worked on a live virus vaccine. Both had advantages and disadvantages. However, Salk was the first to prove his vaccine could help slow the spread of polio. It quickly went into use across the United States and around the world.

EXPLORE ONLINE

Chapter One discusses the widespread fear of polio in the first half of the 1900s. The website below explores the impact the polio virus had on people. As you know, every source is different. What information does the website give about the spread of polio and how people tried to prevent it? How is the information from the website the same as the information in Chapter One? What new information did you learn from the website?

DEFEATING POLIO, THE DISEASE THAT PARALYZED AMERICA
abdocorelibrary.com/polio-vaccine

SALK SAVES LIVES

Jonas Edward Salk spent much of his career working on a cure for polio. After years of hard work and research, he found success. His vaccine stopped the virus in its tracks. Within a year of its release, the number of polio cases in the United States was cut in half. The results were astounding. The vaccine gave people hope of a life without fearing this frightening disease.

Getting Started

Salk was born on October 28, 1914, in New York City. He went to a special school for children who were very smart. Salk liked to read and got very good grades. He wanted

Salk was a virologist, or a scientist who studies viruses.

a career that would let him make a difference in the world.

Salk graduated from the medical program at New York University in 1939. Then, he went to work at Mount Sinai Hospital in New York for three years. In 1942, he took a job at the University of Michigan. It was here that Salk began studying viruses.

Salk began working with Dr. Thomas Francis Jr. Francis had been Salk's mentor at the university. He showed Salk how to make vaccines. Salk went on to research the causes and effects of diseases in 1944.

Making a Move

Salk began studying polio and looking for a cure. Other scientists had made vaccines, but none were successful. Salk wanted to change that.

In 1951, Salk had his first big break in his polio research. He was part of the team that confirmed there were three different types of polio. Salk experimented on a killed virus vaccine for polio. His work caught the

Salk was appointed director of the Virus Research Laboratory at the University of Pittsburg in 1947.

eye of the NFIP. The organization believed Salk's vaccine was the best way to stop polio. The NFIP gave Salk the funds he needed to do his research.

Monkey Business

Salk grew the polio virus on kidney cells he took from monkeys. Then, he killed the virus with a chemical.

Salk used the killed virus to make a vaccine. He injected monkeys with the vaccine to see if it would work. He tested it on thousands of monkeys. His experiment was a success.

Next, Salk needed to test his vaccine on humans. However, no one wanted to be injected with the disease, killed or not. Salk was so sure his vaccine would work that he tested it on himself. He also gave it to his own wife and three children in 1952. He tested it on members of his staff. He also gave it to children at the D. T. Watson Home for Crippled Children who already had the disease. Again, his tests were successful. Salk announced his findings on a radio show in March 1953. It seemed Salk had found a way to stop polio from spreading. But he needed much more proof before the public would agree.

Once the vaccine proved effective on monkeys, Salk could finally test it on humans.

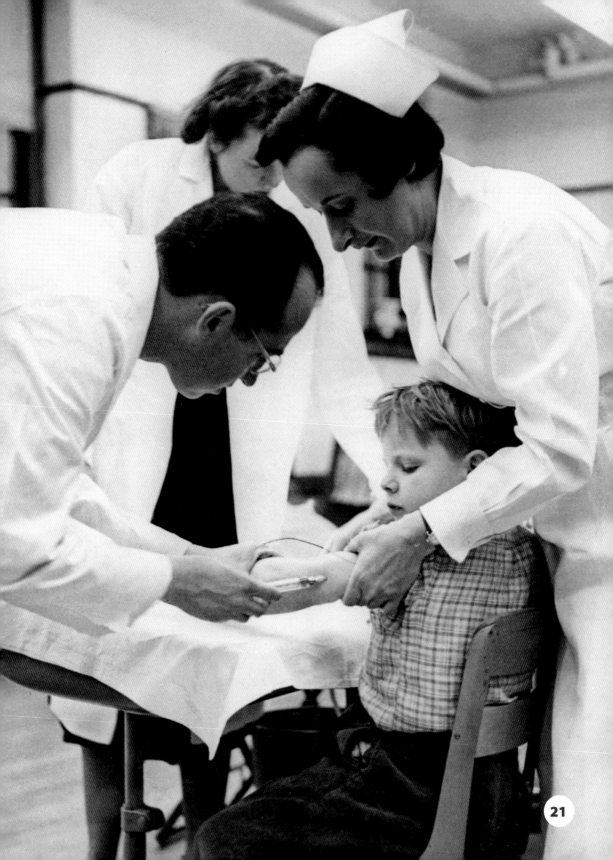

D. T. WATSON HOME

David Thompson Watson was a wealthy businessman. He and his wife, Margaret, spent lots of time and money helping care for children with disabilities. When David died in 1916, the D. T. Watson Home for Crippled Children near Sewickley, Pennsylvania, was founded in his honor. In the 1940s, the home started to take in many children who had polio. In 1952, Salk gave his vaccine to 30 children at the home who already had polio. He wanted to see if it would make the body more immune to the disease. His tests were successful.

Polio Pioneers

Salk began a nationwide test of his vaccine on April 26, 1954. The US Public Health Service approved the trial. The NFIP helped promote it. Children were given three doses over a period of time. Half of the children were given the real vaccine. The other half of the children were given a fake vaccine. If the children who got the real vaccine built up antibodies and the ones who got the fake vaccine did not, Salk would know the vaccine worked. More than

1.8 million children ages 6 to 9 were part of the trial. They became known as the Polio Pioneers. It was the largest clinical trial in US history.

Francis led the trial. A year after it started, the results were in. People all over the world wanted to know if Salk's vaccine had worked. On April 12, 1955, Francis announced the vaccine was safe to use. Salk was a hero. People celebrated the news. Church bells rang and whistles blew in factories. Parents cried tears of joy. The days of locking up their children to protect them from polio were over.

Vaccine Approval

Salk's vaccine was approved for use within hours of the announcement. Millions of orders were placed for it. President Dwight Eisenhower held a special event at the White House in Salk's honor. Seven years after the vaccine went into use, polio cases dropped from approximately 45,000 per year in the United States to less than 1,000.

THE CUTTER INCIDENT

In the spring of 1955, 200,000 children were given a bad batch of the polio vaccine. The virus had not been properly killed. This meant that children were being given the live virus. The vaccine had been made by a company called Cutter Laboratories. Approximately 40,000 children got polio as a result. Of them, approximately 200 became paralyzed and ten died. The vaccination program was stopped for a short time. All of the bad vaccines were destroyed. The government came up with a better way to watch over companies that made the vaccine. The vaccination program started back up again in the fall. No other cases of polio in the United States are known to have been caused by the Salk vaccine.

Salk made the vaccine available for anyone to use. He never made a profit from his discovery. In 1963, Salk founded the Salk Center for Biological Studies. He worked on cures for diseases such as cancer and multiple sclerosis. Salk died of heart failure on June 23, 1995.

STRAIGHT TO THE
SOURCE

On April 22, 1955, President Dwight Eisenhower gave this speech about Salk in honor of his achievement:

The work of Dr. Salk is in the highest tradition of selfless and dedicated medical research. He has provided a means for the control of a dread disease. By helping scientists in other countries . . . by offering to them the strains of seed virus and professional aid so that the production of vaccine can be started by them everywhere . . . Dr. Salk is a benefactor of mankind.

His achievement, a credit to our entire scientific community, does honor to all the people of the United States.

Source: James C. Hagerty. "White House Press Release with Text of Citations Given by the President to Dr. Jonas E. Salk and the National Foundation for Infantile Paralysis." EisenhowerArchives.gov. *Eisenhower Presidential Library, Museum & Boyhood Home,* n.d. Web. January 29, 2018.

Point of View

This text views Salk in a very favorable way. What does it say makes Salk such a standout person? Read back through this chapter. Do you agree? Why or why not?

THE SABIN SOLUTION

While Jonas Salk was hard at work on his killed vaccine, Albert Sabin was working on a live virus vaccine. For years, people had been debating if a live or killed virus was the better choice. Sabin thought only a live virus would offer immunity over a long period of time. He put a great deal of time and effort into proving his theory. But he found it hard to get support for his research. Many people had already put their support behind Salk's vaccine.

Getting Started

Sabin was born in Bialystok, Poland, on August 26, 1906. In 1921, he and his family

Sabin was an expert in microbiology. This is the study of microorganisms, such as bacteria and viruses.

moved to Paterson, New Jersey. After high school, Sabin decided to become a doctor.

Sabin got a scholarship to pay for his schooling. He lived in a room at Harlem Hospital in New York City. He paid for it by doing odd jobs around the hospital. One of his jobs was identifying different types of pneumonia in patients. He found a new method for quickly typing up his reports. It helped save lives. The method was named after Sabin. Other doctors took notice of his work.

Early Accomplishments

Sabin got his degree in medicine in 1931. He decided to work for his mentor, Dr. William H. Park, over the summer. Sabin studied bacteria in Park's lab. At that time there was a huge polio outbreak in New York City. It was one of the worst ever. Park urged Sabin to research the disease. Sabin's work earned him a great deal of respect from other doctors.

Sabin used chimpanzees in the early parts of his experiments.

By 1939, Sabin was known as a brilliant researcher. He had many achievements to his name. Sabin had written dozens of papers on research topics for journals. He discovered a type of virus known as the B virus. He was also part of a team that proved the polio virus could grow in human tissue in a lab.

Many people wanted to work with Sabin. He went on to work at the Cincinnati Children's Hospital Research Foundation.

Polio Research

Sabin wasted no time setting up his lab. He jumped right into researching the polio virus. To date, most research had been done on tissues from monkeys. Instead, Sabin used brain tissue from human embryos. Most people believed the polio virus got into the body through the nose. Sabin found that it went through the digestive tract. It was a major discovery.

Soon after, Sabin began looking into a live virus vaccine for polio. Sabin believed this type of vaccine

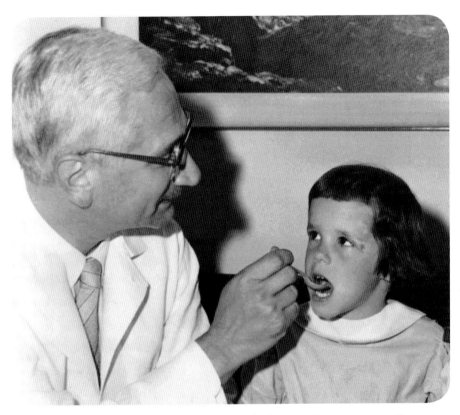

Most children preferred receiving their vaccinations orally rather than through a needle.

would offer longer-lasting immunity than a killed virus vaccine. Sabin also thought an oral vaccine would be better than one that is injected. He thought it was easier to give to people. He began to grow and test the virus in tissues and animals.

Sabin thought Salk's killed virus plan for a vaccine was not as good as his own live virus plan. He wanted to take his time to find what he felt was the best solution to the problem of polio. But people were eager to stop the disease as soon as possible. Salk's research was moving at a much faster pace than Sabin's.

Sabin finally found a vaccine he thought worked well. He started testing it on people. He gave it to himself, his wife, his two children, and other researchers in 1957. He also tested it on hundreds of prisoners. The tests were successful.

PERSPECTIVES

BASIL O'CONNOR AND MARCH OF DIMES

On January 3, 1938, President Roosevelt founded the NFIP to help raise funds for the polio research. He asked his friend Basil O'Connor to run the organization. Even ten cents would make a difference, they were told. It would create a "march of dimes to reach all the way to the White House." Letters poured in. By January 29, the White House had received 2,680,000 dimes. By the late 1940s, the NFIP was raising $50 million a year for polio. O'Connor used the money to set up programs for vaccine research.

While polio victims waited anxiously for the vaccine, they found comfort in different kinds of physical therapies, such as water therapy.

Soviet Support

By 1957, the World Health Organization (WHO) wanted Sabin to start mass trials of his vaccine. But it was hard to find support in the United States. Salk's vaccine was already being widely tested across the country. Sabin looked to other countries around the world for support instead. From 1957 to 1959, Sabin's

SABIN VACCINE INSTITUTE

Plans for the Sabin Vaccine Institute were in place before Sabin died. He was first told about it in October 1992. Dr. Herman R. Shepherd, the head of Armstrong Pharmaceuticals, started the institute. He wanted to honor Sabin for his lifelong work in virus research. He sent a letter to Sabin telling him about his plans. Today, the nonprofit organization is focused on education and research. It also develops new vaccines.

vaccine was tested on 10 million people in the Soviet Union. It was also tested on millions of people in Chile, Holland, Sweden, England, Japan, Singapore, and the Czech Republic.

The tests were all successful. By 1960, Sabin's vaccine was approved for use in the United States. It soon became the vaccine of choice across the country. It was also recommended by WHO for use around the world.

Sabin's vaccine was easy to use and it lasted a lifetime. It also gave complete immunity. Most importantly, it was much cheaper than Salk's vaccine.

This was a key factor for countries that did not have a lot of money to fight the disease. Sabin's vaccine was used to get rid of polio in most countries around the world.

After the polio vaccine, Sabin spent many years researching cancer. He thought it might be caused by a virus. In 1977, he decided it was not. He died of heart failure on March 3, 1993. The Sabin Vaccine Institute was founded in his honor later that year.

FURTHER EVIDENCE

Chapter Three talks about Albert Sabin's polio vaccine trials, including those in the Soviet Union. What was one of the main points of this chapter? What evidence is included to support this point? Read the article at the website below. Does the information on the website support the main point of the chapter? Does it present new evidence?

US-RUSSIA PARTNERSHIP: DEVELOPING THE POLIO VACCINE
abdocorelibrary.com/polio-vaccine

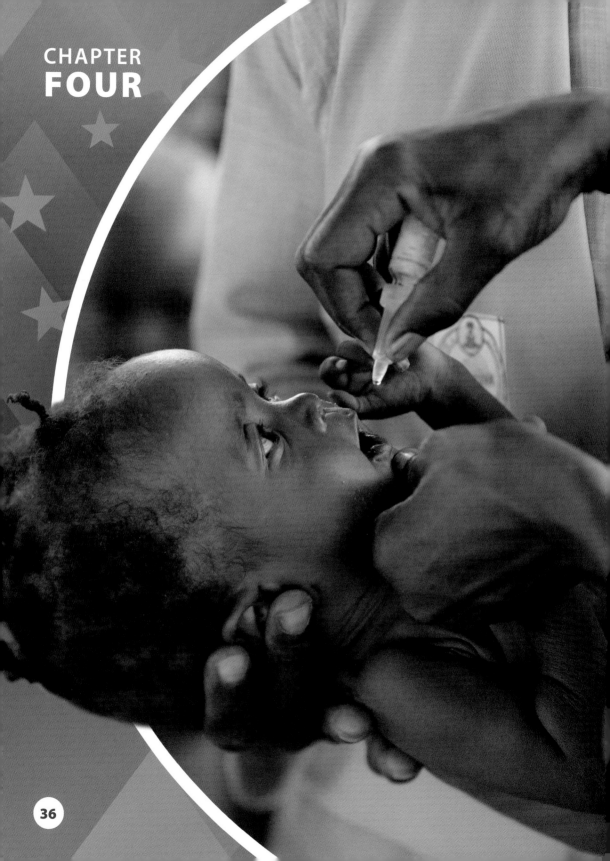

GLOBAL POLIO ERADICATION INITIATIVE

I n 1988, the Global Polio Eradication Initiative (GPEI) started. National governments and five international organizations came together. They wanted to try to stop the spread of polio in all parts of the world. Since then, more than 2.5 billion children have been vaccinated. Polio cases have been reduced by 99.9 percent.

Salk versus Sabin

By 1963, it seemed the debate between Salk's and Sabin's vaccines was over. Sabin's vaccine was being used to fight polio in most parts

UNICEF is one of the organizations working with the Global Polio Eradication Initiative to help eliminate polio throughout the world.

POLIO TODAY

- Polio is at most risk of outbreak in three countries today: Nigeria, Afghanistan, and Pakistan. They have not been able to stop the virus from spreading.

- One of the three types of polio viruses has not been seen since 2015.

- Two countries had polio outbreaks in 2017: Democratic Republic of the Congo and Syria. They had previously stopped the virus but are facing re-infection.

- There were 17 countries at risk of polio outbreaks in 2017.

- In 1988, there were 350,000 cases of polio worldwide. By 2016, there were only 37.

- The killed polio vaccine is 90 percent effective after two doses. It is 99 percent effective after three doses.

- One out of 2.7 million children will become paralyzed by Sabin's vaccine.

While treating the disease has come a long way since it was first diagnosed, there are still countries that are threatened by polio outbreaks today.

of the world. By 1994, there were no more polio cases in the Western Hemisphere. The only new cases were those caused by the vaccine itself. They were very rare.

In 1999, a US federal advisory group recommended going back to Salk's vaccine. They said there was too much of a risk of infecting a person with polio using Sabin's live virus vaccine. Another advisory board made the same suggestion in 2009. The debate is ongoing today.

Going Forward

The GPEI uses statistics and facts about which vaccines work best in different situations to decide when the Salk or Sabin vaccine should be used. In some places, the risk of polio is very high. The virus needs to be contained quickly. The GPEI mainly uses Sabin's vaccine because it is cheap and easy to use. In polio-free nations where there is low risk, the Salk vaccine is used. It has no risk of paralysis.

Someday, the GPEI hopes polio will no longer be a problem. In the meantime, the organization is looking for ways to make Salk's vaccine cheaper to use.

PERSPECTIVES
MODERN RESEARCH

With the polio virus nearly gone, many researchers have stopped studying it. They feel there is no longer a need. But others believe there is good reason for them to keep up their work. Scientists can apply what they know about the polio virus to stop other similar viruses. They could help find new ways to treat and cure viruses such as Ebola, Zika, and the flu.

PROTECTING AGAINST POLIO

To date, polio still has no cure. The only way to prevent it is to protect against it. The best way to do so is by getting the polio vaccine. In the United States, most people get the vaccine when they are children. They have a series of four doses of Salk's killed virus vaccine. They get the first dose when they are just two months old. They have the final dose when they start school. Adults who have a high risk for polio and were vaccinated as children can get a booster shot of Salk's vaccine. This will ensure they are protected for life. A booster is recommended for people who plan to visit places that still have polio. It is also given to adults who care for people who may be carrying the polio virus or who work with the virus in labs.

The GPEI also has plans in place to contain outbreaks if they occur.

The GPEI is planning for a polio-free world. It is planning to use polio facilities for other causes. It is also working with labs to help contain the virus. Thanks to the work of Salk and Sabin, the GPEI has hopes that one day, polio will be gone forever.

STRAIGHT TO THE
SOURCE

The Bill and Melinda Gates foundation is committed to working with the GPEI and other organizations around the world to eliminate Polio forever. In the foundation's annual letter, Gates talks about why he and his wife believe getting rid of Polio is so important:

> It's thrilling to be nearing the day when no children will be crippled by polio. But we're often asked why we're making such a big effort on polio if our priority is to save lives. The answer is, ending polio will save lives—through the magic of zero. When polio is eradicated, the world can dedicate polio funds to improving child health, and the lessons from polio will lead to better immunization systems for other diseases.

Source: Bill and Melinda Gates. "Our 2017 Annual Letter: Warren Buffet's Best Investment." *Gatesnotes.com*. The Gates Notes, LLC, February 14, 2017. Web. January 29, 2018.

What's the Big Idea?
Read the excerpt from Gates's annual letter carefully. What is the main idea of the passage? Name two pieces of evidence in the passage that support this idea.

IMPORTANT
DATES

1894
The first polio epidemic happens in the United States.

1910s
Polio is widespread across the country.

1921
In August, politician and future US president Franklin D. Roosevelt is diagnosed with polio.

1938
On January 3, President Roosevelt creates the NFIP to help raise funds for polio research and care.

1942
Salk takes a job at the University of Michigan and begins studying viruses.

1951
Salk discovers there are three different types of polio.

1952
Salk begins testing his vaccine on himself, his wife, and their three children.

1954
Salk begins a nationwide test of his vaccine on
April 26.

1955
On April 12, Thomas Francis Jr. announces that Salk's
vaccine is safe to use.

1955 to 1957
Sabin successfully tests his vaccine on hundreds of prisoners.

1957 to 1959
Sabin successfully tests his vaccine on 10 million people in
the Soviet Union and millions of others around the world.

1960
Sabin's vaccine is approved for use in the United States.

1979
North America is declared polio free.

1988
The Global Polio Eradication Initiative (GPEI)
is launched.

STOP AND
THINK

Tell the Tale

Imagine you are listening on the radio when the announcer states that a polio vaccine has been discovered. How would you feel after hearing the announcement? Write 200 words about your reaction.

Surprise Me

Chapter One discusses how polio spreads. After reading this book, what two or three facts about polio did you find most surprising? Write a few sentences about each fact. Why did you find each fact surprising?

Dig Deeper

After reading this book, what questions do you still have about polio? With an adult's help, find a few reliable sources that can help you answer your questions. Write a paragraph about what you learned.

GLOSSARY

central nervous system
the brain, spinal cord, and tissues that control thought, movement, and sensation

contagious
able to spread quickly from one person to another through contact

contaminated
made impure through contact or mixing with something else

immune system
the cells, tissues, proteins, and organs that work together to fight off disease, infection, and germs

paralysis
a loss of movement of a part of the body

pneumonia
a disease where the lungs are inflamed

quarantine
to keep a person away from other people

theory
a guess that is supported by evidence

vaccine
a substance that helps protect against disease

ONLINE
RESOURCES

To learn more about the discovery of the polio vaccine, visit our free resource websites below.

Core Library CONNECTION
FREE! COMMON CORE MULTIMEDIA RESOURCES

Visit **abdocorelibrary.com** for free Common Core resources for teachers and students, including vetted activities, multimedia, and booklinks, for deeper subject comprehension.

Booklinks NONFICTION NETWORK
FREE! ONLINE NONFICTION RESOURCES

Visit **abdobooklinks.com** for free additional online weblinks for further learning. These links are routinely monitored and updated to provide the most current information available.

LEARN
MORE

Hand, Carol. *Vaccines*. Minneapolis, MN: Abdo Publishing, 2014.

Llanas, Sheila. *Jonas Salk: Medical Innovator and Polio Vaccine Developer*. Minneapolis, MN: Abdo Publishing, 2014.

ABOUT THE AUTHORS

Duchess Harris, JD, PhD

Professor Harris is the chair of the American Studies department at Macalester College and curator of the Duchess Harris Collection of ABDO books. She is the author and coauthor of recently released ABDO books including *Hidden Human Computers: The Black Women of NASA*, *Black Lives Matter*, and *Race and Policing*.

Before working with ABDO, she authored several other books on the topics of race, culture, and American history. She served as an associate editor for *Litigation News*, the American Bar Association Section of Litigation's quarterly flagship publication, and was the first editor in chief of *Law Raza*, an interactive online journal covering race and the law, published at William Mitchell College of Law. She has earned a PhD in American Studies from the University of Minnesota and a JD from William Mitchell College of Law.

Heather C. Hudak

Heather C. Hudak has written hundreds of books for children and edited thousands more. She loves learning about new topics, traveling the world, and spending time with her husband and many pets.

INDEX